NO SPACE BUT

Also by Joy Howard

SECOND BITE
(with Hilary J Murray and Gina Shaw)

A TWIST OF MALICE (ed)

EXIT MOONSHINE

CRACKING ON (ed)

NO SPACE BUT THEIR OWN

New Poems about Birds

Edited by Joy Howard
Illustrations: Emma Stansfield

GREY HEN

First published in 2010 by Grey Hen Press
PO Box 450
Keighley
West Yorkshire
BD22 9WS
www.greyhenpress.com

ISBN 978-0-9552952-5-6

Printed by GB Winstonmead, Loughborough, Leicestershire LE11 1LE

Special thanks are due to Bill Kenmir of the RSPB for his knowledgeable and insightful comments throughout the preparation of this book.

Poetry is like a bird, it ignores all frontiers.

Yevgeny Yevtushenko

Preface

Birds have always inspired art – images of birds can be found from the earliest times. They are seen both as omens and as rescuers. They symbolise love, hope and above all, freedom. In this book, poets writing today seek to examine and celebrate our complex involvement with the lives of birds. These poems reflect the ancient myths and personifications that still inhabit our modern minds and at the same time speak to the intensely personal nature of encounters in the present. Some focus on the impact that connections with birds have on our lives, others on the unique qualities of each species. This is a collection of poems and artwork that should strike a chord with all bird-lovers, and contribute to winning over those who have yet to be entranced.

Joy Howard

Contents

Air

Endpiece

Foreword

A great many things have changed for birds in the last twenty years or so. Their lives have generally become more perilous (climate change, global warming, industrialisation) and the value we put on them - and the interest we take in them - has correspondingly increased. Whereas the man and woman in the street might have thought 'bird-watching' a slightly pitiable activity a generation back, now 'birding' is widely respected - even envied.

At the same time, the amount of attention given to birds in poetry has risen sharply. Not just to how they look, fly, eat, feed, breed and call, but to the ways in which they prove both the delight and the danger of existence. That's to say: birds have become increasingly admirable and increasingly admonitory - while also being increasingly looked-up-to for the things they are in themselves.

This excellent anthology proves the point. It is full of poems that are good at looking exactly, while remaining conscious that what they see has a place in the larger scheme of things. Above all, they are impressively sensitive to the ways in which birds belong in our lives and yet are fundamentally different and beyond us. It deserves a large and enthusiastic readership.

Andrew Motion

Prologue

Assembly of Birds

Ardrossan and above the chinking masts
of the weekend sailboats, against a light
already dimmer-switched, before the moon
turns on full power, black flecks
like giant ash-flakes from some conflagration
too huge to think are tossed around the sky –

there is a pattern but not ours, the same
unvoiced consent as in a flock of pigeons
suddenly rising and wheeling and settling
on a rooftop, then off, veering widdershins back
and then the whole manoeuvre over again,
seemingly just for the hell

for we haven't a clue any more than we know
what the geese in the topfield near the road to Rothesay
parley about in their urgent patois
hundreds milling around as if in waiting
for some long-heralded event: for sure
it's not about us. We're unnoticed

just like the time we sat watching the constant
flicker and dart of pinkbreast chaffinches,
seizing their tiny beakfuls of nut and seed
speeding home to their nests as if they would never
forage again – then back in a couple of minutes,
intricate ballet choreographed on the wing.

Parallel lives at the edge of attention
which every so often startle us out of our doze:
be it the laughter of townbred gulls
still harsh with the rasp of the sea, a swan in sail
or migrant swifts arranging themselves
in perfect chords on a stave of telegraph wires.

A C Clarke

Land

Early Music

The five-o'clock blackbird bursts the bubble of my dream.
He forges a thin gold chain that slinks across the tiles
and coils into my cortexes.
More skilled than many guests at Ronnie Scott's,
he endlessly elaborates his simple themes
with a distinctive vocal fingerprint.
Can this virtuoso be the one from last year and before?
Or is the melodic assay mark passed down
like an eyebrow quirk
or Grandad's gold half-hunter on its weighty fob
To my belovèd Husband Arthur curlicued in the back?
Does each fledgling generation pick this treasure up,
work variations of its own?
The watch is silent in its velvet nest behind socks and handkerchiefs,
while the fantasias are free to be admired
(except in the grudging dawn) by everyone.

Gill Learner

Hedge Sparrows

I picked July to do it, hoping the young
would have flown the nests. My arms a thicket
of scratches, I stood back to admire
my handiwork, the destruction of a village.

The sparrows were out that morning.
I watched them return, perch on a broken twig,
an amputated stump. They had a bath
and assessed the situation.

No two ways about it, home was gone.
No sheltering branches left, no arm of berries
to see them through the winter. They'd been counting
on that bough sticking out of the wheelie-bin.

They'd hoped to bed down in the warm feathers
of that rough basket. Now they bob from perch
to perch like those couples on Location, Location
who can never quite decide about the view.

Carole Bromley

The Wren Doesn't Wait for May

Unlovely, hawthorn squats through winter;
rattles its thorns to defy the wind.
It flaunts a ragged crown of stolen tatters;
scraps of fur and feather, shreds of frayed plastic.

A brown blur shutters through the shabby
tangle, ups tail, flicks from branch to barb.
Her feathers lift in the wind and she darts a canny eye
to scan for insect bounty. Head cocked, she hears
her suitors throw out liquid trills to tempt
her; she opens her throat and sings:
for the moment, for the wren, for the thorn.

Angela France

Owls at Midnight

No carol singers swinging lanterns
this year, but singing nonetheless.
I lift you in Barbie pyjamas, dough-
warm, and bring you to the window.

Two owls call: one squats on our chimney,
a cottage-loaf swivelling necklessly.
The other is in the trees, the far side
of the field, past the silo, over the stream.

Each time the far one calls, the near one
elongates and whistles like a steam train;
then, in the answering silence, he trembles
his whole body, waiting for the female

from her wood post, before her wondering call
comes again, and he whoos with all
the bagpipe of his gut. Call, overlap,
overlap, call, lose sequence, take it back.

'Look,' I say, 'look.' But you are tired,
your head is drooping against my head.
Owls have no power for you, any more
than 'Good King Wenceslas' last year.

There are foxes in the garden, and voles
make fragile tunnels through the grass.
I take you to bed, heavy with sleep.
The garden is silent. Something cries.

Marianne Burton

Monday Morning

ice at the station

jackdaw patrols the white line
at the edge of the platform

flops down
to check the rails

all the while eyeing you
eyeing you

as though he knows something
as though he knows

you shiver

Gina Shaw

No Contest

Who says the days of chivalry
are gone? While she, clad in the green

of beech before it coppers, feeds
discreetly on seeds, he waits until

the sun brings forth his rival.
No coward, for all the white on his wings,

with beak turned lance he flies
straight at him, aims for the feathered

helmet of slate-blue. No match for glass.
It is himself the chaffinch sees: elusive suitor

sporting the muted colours of his lady's favour.
          Wiped out by a cloud.

Kathryn Daszkiewicz

Marsh Tits on the Wrekin

Birds, like leaves,
As if you had taken
And shaken the tree,
And out had fluttered,
Had tumbled and swayed
Their way to the ground,
These drunken revellers,
Little brown carousers,
Scoop and sweep like a florin
Dropped in the ocean;
Then caught by the updraught,
Surf the breeze and are whisked, transplanted
To the next tree -
Air layering of birds -
Till a startle shakes their roots loose
And they leapfrog down
To rustle for grubs on the ground.

Hermione Sandall

New Season's Blackbird

Oh you've got the full eye now, clown,
round as a bell with an orange rim,
straight up. No fooling now, half dressed
and shying at starlings. Turned up male
and black as the bottom of a well.
Eyeing me sidelong with a birdlook,
or one of me. You'd have to turn
to see the other but you won't.
If a devil looks out from anything
it's you, snook cocked in scorched leaves.
You couldn't care less for heatwaves in your
silky gear, shimmying out of the lawn
cool as Sharif on his camel.
Here's looking at you, yellow beak.
Welcome to the intemperate zone.

Pamela Coren

Goldfinch

Never at rest
feeding on seeds as fine as dust
a freeze-frame life of flickering shadows
in the blur and brash of day.

Black bonneted, querulous head,
tossing seed skins into the wind,
a mask of yellow and red
gold flash, open wing.

Brown as a fading bruise
a finger print over the heart,
as if this bird had once been caught
and the hand had left its mark.

Lynn Alderson

Crow on the Roof

a thicket of rain bars
the way to the bus stop

up on a roof-ridge
a huge crow squats motionless

he counts the drops
computes the downpour

a brandished umbrella
will not thwart him

he won't let
the sun shine yet

Gina Shaw

The Collared Doves

Since their table was moved the birds
have abandoned us – odd to wake
without their *caroo, croo, croo* – collared doves,
the same two, picking corn out of the wild bird food;

the rush of their wings, a soft flop on wood
then all day, small flurries and whirrs as they swoop,
land, preen and chunter, scatter seed and take off.

So we coax them back, lay a trail
of sweet corn from the wall where the old table was
to the new. But it stays untouched

or is raided by strutting magpies
then jackdaws, squabbling and raucous;
the bright flash of a jay. We love his colour.

But it's the doves we wait for, pearl grey,
a black ring at the throat; their croon
of content bubbled through our sleep.

And they don't migrate, these doves, no,
except as they come and go through the green
of our woods, the sky's shifting blue

and bring both feathered through last summer's leaves,
morning's half light, the white glare of the sun;
themselves from the dark back to us.

Jo Haslam

A Wintering Lark

A den of grass, a lair of stems;
and what does he eat, the lark in winter
crouched in his breath, his blown husk
of feather, heart like a seed?

Who knows if he will make it through?
No inkling of flight or song –
I think forgetting saves him,
claws meshed in sheltered ground.

Let me be motionless
so fear won't jolt him; suffer
waiting as the lark does, balanced
in unforced stillness while the time

finds its own pulse. Held in this chill
we are thinnest glass: test it
with a fingertip for latent music
and it may sing or shatter.

M R Peacocke

The Blackbird Sings

Rain has rinsed all gloom
from the sky. The garden
breathes and stretches.

The lawn preens itself.
Skeins of green swirl up
into a gold-tipped conifer.

The sun, which was not
drowned, consents to perform
its old trick with the light.

House, tree, grass, are
gilded, enchanted, spelled
under a net of song.

Gina Shaw

Chaffinch

That's me. Little jackpot, dash
of a gentle rainbow. Unexpected.
I almost look exotic, yet I'm so small
I can fit inside a hedge, hide
behind a large lime leaf. You might not see
me, as you tramp through the woods
with your strange songs of creaking words,
your loud drinks and rustling bags of food.

I am still here. Quick as a twitch,
wild genie of the countryside's
green bottle. Free as all flying creatures,
skimming the sky with my rose petal belly.
Scooping up air with my monochrome wings
as if I were gathering to me
all of the summer. Keeping alive the story
of the slow dance of the seasons.
A jewellery box of sparkling memories
for those who treasure such things.

Fiona Durance

Arrivals

Heads cocked to one side, feathered
shoulders hunched, our neighbours watch them
arrive, one quiet Sunday. Breaking
the estate's rules, they flash
metallic colours, arch scarlet feet,
dull the magpie's fresh paint,
spilt-petrol sheen of starlings.

Nineteen altogether - racing,
spitting, shrieking like soprano crows -
ready to pillage the whole district.

Spun glass shapes in the sycamore
swaying in its rustling yellow
tossing spent keys down in showers -
or in the crab-apple, one red foot
curled round a branch, one round a fruit,
hooked beaks chewing.

For days I think they'll vanish, until
I find them listed in the local guides -
ring-necked, resident for generations.
Not that they care:

across the sky they dive in twos or threes
their sirens blaring
then hurl themselves to rest, folding their jade.

Christine Webb

Sparrowhawk

As we came from the back door, an arrow
- of thrush, or blackbird, or bullfinch - shot

from quince tree to thorn bush, tight-trailing,
as a child's kite draws its paper tail, a hawk,

which slammed, clawed feet first, into the spikes,
while lunch wriggled through a hole to freedom.

For fifteen seconds it lay crucified -
wings museum-fixed, spread-eagled by thorns -

as we watched our exhibit twist against
its pivot, its spine pull against the pinioning,

eyes extruding, beak gaping, tongue protruding,
barred feathers pinned wide for our inspection.

Then, sucking back like a tide, it unstuck, flew
straight as a catapult's slug, sharp past the gate,

leaving us piecing together what we'd seen
with what we would claim later we had seen.

Marianne Burton

Ubiquitous

Scorched by the fire of Gehenna,
he likes a fight.
His war cry sounds
day and evening.
Solitary, he attacks
to defend his territory.
He courts, mates, and repels
intruders in a rage.
Sometimes bigamous
his beady black eyes rove.

His tic tac scolding
is silent in July.
He will catch a bee, pick off
its sting, crush its head
and swallow it whole.
In the dusk snatches insects
round streetlamps and moths
at lighted windows.
In winter he may die of cold.
The cat which kills and devours
him, will vomit him up.

Jenny Morris

Owl Calls

(*The owl calls the name of the one who will die next* – Trad.)

Owl sails over. Who-who-ing floats
into the night: whose name? Under
roofs, under that soundless sweep, hearts
half stop. The starfish-handed

baby, air scalding the raw lungs,
gasps; on the stairs, leg doubled
back, an elder waits out the long
hours. And I wake too, the bubble

of sound breaking as I surface,
listen to the wave of your breath,
my hand riding the fall and rise
of your ribs. Safe. We both

drift away. The owl moves on
over the houses. The stars listen.

Christine Webb

Hawk on a Chimney Pot

A difficult perspective to guess
from the ground. Her brown
speckles hunch among terracotta towers.
Fields of raindark slate tilt
to geometric horizons. Rain smokes
round her shoulders. Rags of sky
catch in twittering electronic twigs.

Her eye swivels like Hubble.
In one pane she sights a black speck
moving on a square of lighter ground.

She carries ticks on her quills,
like dark seed pearls, arthritis,
cold watchfulness in a limited sky
and I carry her wicked eye
pursed up in my drawstring heart.

Chittering quietly she gathers herself.
Her shoulders peak like wire hangers,
parachute silk wings rip out,
one balletic twiddle and her thick
talons shove her off the roof.

Some creature will suffer her
today like the black clap
of silence before a bomb.

Kate Foley

Dunnock

(Lines in italics are taken from the RSPB Guide to British Birds)

sometimes it sings sweet and soft
    [*song: a weak pleasant jingle*]
not four feet away in the hedge

but it's not that

it skims the fence and shrubs
    [*flight: usually low and over a short distance*]
judging the clearance by millimetres

no not that either

it's no robin redbreast or blue tit
it might at first glance be a sparrow
    [*streaked back and grey head and underparts*]
but there's none of that squabbling gregariousness

so… what…?

it flits in and out under the bushes
    [*habitat: hedgerows, bushy areas, scrub, open woods with undergrowth*]
hardly noticeable
getting on with its own business

plain

unpretentious

that's it

the dunnock

Gina Shaw

Rooks in February

The rookery jabbers with committees
debating sites, dimensions, settling
the status of new arrivals, authorising
repairs to wreckage of nests. Over and over
they adjourn, to soar up in a chackle
of voices, review the parishes below.

First they enact some laws for the spring:
rain to fall next Tuesday, softening the crust
of frost; daffodils after a further ten days'
extension to begin hardening, swelling
with seed; east winds to veer southwards
by the month's end.

Now with hoarse urgency
they move the next business: judging the souls
of the recently dead. They deliberate,
pronounce. Their language is technical,
their verdicts obscure: what is the sentence
they call, call, down from the grey sky?

Christine Webb

Haunt

When the trees were cut back, the owls moved off
leaving us restless for nights. We'd sleep fitful,
one ear half-cocked for the mournful cry –
the loneliest thing we'd heard those months
of trouble and chaos. Strange how we missed them,
ghost companions, reminders of loss. We'd wake
in the dark – four or five – to a breathless silence.

They came back at last – July,
when I heard that call unstitch the night,
a stone's throw from our open window.
I thought of the stories of luck and signs,
creatures made up, like us, of cells,
tissue and blood, but aerial, mysterious,
beating the bounds from the first birch tree
at the edge of our woods, to the low
dense shrub that borders our garden

And I thought we were blessed to have them again
and know we weren't alone in the world
just humankind, with no haunted bird
to tug our nerve endings, remind us
who we are or were, or nudge us through dreams
where we glide with their ease. And their secret life
went on in the dark while we slept as if
it was safe after all, and into our range
the echoing night whose acres they trawl.

Jo Haslam

When the Wren Sings

When the wren sings its round body is a mouth
opening at a beak. A wired radius,
it points sonic needles upwards and outwards.
Where it is it becomes song. Streets away
it clips idlers who start, stare around for aliens.
What planet it comes from is beyond reach,
tucked in a thorn turret. King secret,
it is green inside, for bugs. Once, twice it appears,
oscillating on spiny feet, switches back inside
in a glance. Signals flood the scope
and yes, it says, yes, there is, there is.

Pamela Coren

Water

Kittiwakes

(from *Dunstanburgh*)

In the city of kittiwakes everyone's scolding
The comings and goings,
The restless arrivals,
Departures, the shuffling
To-ings and fro-ings;

With their clean yellow beaks,
Their iron-grey backs,
Salt-white breasts
And their wings dipped in darkness.

White wings of a kittiwake
Shear off the cliff
In a deep sickle dive
Into empty air
To soar, and circle.

And back comes the babble -
Peremptory cries
That rise to a higher, angrier echo -
Angular splashes against the slow
Undertone of the sea.

And he's back again,
To elaborate greetings:
Head-shaking,
Billing,
Fencing twin beaks,
Excitedly weaving two heads back and forward
While everyone shrieks,
And the entire city
Grinds into gear to announce the arrival.

A snowstorm of kittiwakes, shaken, won't settle,
In the shanty-town,
In the high-rise huddle,
The tenement squalor,
The squabble and babble...

Katrina Porteous

Haiku

There sails the heron,
drawing behind him a long
wake of solitude.

M R Peacocke

Bodybuilding for Beginners

They stand in water, exercising wings
in tight formation. As feathers replace down
they flex their growing muscles, learn to reach
up to the sky. As bodies bulk, the reps
increase. Their trainer, mother eider duck,
encourages her brood. The choppy waves
a moving platform for their awkward moves,
they flop and fall, shake feathers out and flap
until instinctive balance wins its round
with gravity. The training session ends.
The ducklings paddle slowly out to sea
to sit on water, bobbing in the swell.

Lyn Moir

In the Wild

I've not seen you, though
some declare they have.
Kingfisher. Blue ripple,
how you tax my heart,
darting, fickle tail-feather.

Why do you always
depart just before I
arrive with this torrent
of hope jack-knifing
through my ribcage?

Back home in a stable of
wood and straw, short
on brick, I harbour jays
of insufficient blue,
a tawny owl not keen

on daybreak, and sand
martins whose tenure
of low red cliffs has
trickled away. If I open
the wicket-gate they

soar, brave all elements.
But you are elemental.
Blue lightning, you sear
the eyeball. You fox
senses ranging deeper than

any dull vision I might
possess. Waterfalls were
never your haunt. My
race to discover you
here, a fond mistake.

So I'm off; to contend
with your invisibility,
your wildness, your
beauty, by some quiet
forgotten millpond.

Hilary J Murray

Heron

Iconic bird, along with kingfisher, swallow,
owl, the lark and lapwing,
every poet writes of you. They say you're
hunched by the water,
deep in contemplation,
you *raise the extending ladder of your neck,*
walk on the tall stilts of your legs.
Etc., etc.

Enough of all that stuff! You're nothing but
a sword, a spear, lethal harpoon.
As God, or whoever it was, decided
in his wisdom, or whatever it was,
to make you.

Gill McEvoy

Mallard

Beady-eyed wide-boy, cheerful polymath
Who's never quite as good at anything
As anybody else. Oh, he can fly
But not as the swift flies, not as the kestrel.
He gets there, though, after his own fashion,
And he can swim, but not as the swan swims.
Even his scavenging is overshadowed
By that of gulls, his small predations by
The lordly heron. His are little skills
Thoughtlessly exhibited ad infinitum
In his own idiosyncratic world.
I asked him once, 'Mallard, my feathered friend,
What do you do, exactly? What are you *for*?'
His reply was a wink and a wet shrug;
'Oh, you know, Squire – bit of this, bit of that;
Bit of ducking and diving. Grab what's going.
Know what I mean, Squire, eh? Know what I mean?'

Ann Drysdale

Manx Shearwaters

Meet the wind: walk a headland
to its salt-stung edge
where the known world drops away
to a width of silver
and Skokholm dots the west.

Out across the shine, the arêtes
of the waves, shearwaters are gliding.
Precise, slow, dancing
the air into new shapes,
lathing the sea's grey heave.

Black backs, white bellies, angels
braced in a long-armed cross.
Now soot, now snow, they trail
one wing-tip, then the other,
write their script in the sea.

They quest for shoals, mauve
shadows. Drop to their nests
as night falls. Clutch at rocks,
shunt into barrows, each one
screeching like a fallen bat.

The Norsemen feared them,
heard them wail on the flap of the wind,
their cries pitched between menace
and terror, and the night swinging
on its hinges as if it was damned.

Lynne Wycherley

Teifi Gorge: September

The sky's too flat
too monotone
to practise painting clouds

the sides of the gorge
glutinous green
as shag-pile carpet.

I show you how to make grey –
wetting slate
rubbing two pieces together.

Three swans fly over
and head down-river.
They roar like dragons

shift formation
burn off grey veils.
Their crowns flame gold.

Joan Poulson

Brent Geese

(from *The Refuge Box*)

Slanting over the Sneuk, over
Goswick, that sky-writing, ominous, ancient,
Far away, frightening, almost

Legible. Whose hand, whose voice
Whispers over vast distances, ice

Creaking in it, snow?

No one. But for miles at the tide's edge, geese –
Dark straggles of them, raise

Oaths, hymns, gutturals; and Fenham,
Stirring in its sleep,

In its own rank, spicy smells, its dribbles,
Its ooze, its salt-juices, its tidal creaks,

Opens itself to the sky, to the world, absorbs
Streams, strings of cells pouring

Down from nowhere into one dark body –
A rabble, a squabble, a whole hullabaloo
Trying to make sense of its singleness, an orchestra

Tuning its thousand primitive instruments,
Half bagpipe, half trumpet.

Katrina Porteous

Half a Morning

at 9.30 heron stands
in the middle of the paddock
one leg raised ready

he's deserted the river
its swirls and eddies
its dreams of fish

he could be a carving
lime-washed wood picked out in black
stuck on a pole

at 11 o'clock
he's still there
sighting down his long beak

has he counted off all the frogs
has he even changed legs
what has he done with time

Gina Shaw

The Arctic Terns of Northmavine

I think of them riding the heights,
the earth's blue roll, as if they track
invisible threads, silken and magnetic.

They cross the tropics, Spain, Finisterre
to Shetland's sage-brown fragments in the sea.
Their flecks stoop towards Ronas Hill

and in this place that has no swallows, they arrive
like a gift or a grace – summer spirits
from perpetual snow, the southern pack-ice.

I listen to the sound of their sand-paper tongues,
I glimpse the white sun on their wings,
their vanes half-translucent to heaven.

Fierce with life, how they swerve and dive,
wings snapping open like Japanese fans,
sword-masters feinting with the sea.

All summer they cry – *keeyaar,*
their strident voices grazing the air
until they return to the sky's bright path –

silent atoms on a flickered breath.

Lynne Wycherley

Waymarks

Not a goose in sight
but all around are signs
of last night's roosting,

half a mile
of sea-smoothed sand studded
with droppings, the dune edge

flecked with feathers,
scatterings of breast down
heaped in hollows, filling

the small spaces
between sand sedge
and sun-bleached driftwood,

or trapped on tips of marram,
a flurry of restless pennants
fluttering.

Mavis Gulliver

Bewick's Swans Arrive at Ouse Washes

Just when I think the winter has won,
a black book closing

on pages of light,
and the darkness sways on its haunches

like an impatient bear
scooping up silver minnows,

I sense an agitation in the sky,
long Vs trailing like pennons.

Altocirrus, the swans are as white
as the tundra they come from.

Their cries multiply. Their bodies
crash-land on the water

star after star after star.

Lynne Wycherley

How to Watch a Seagull

The parent birds must build a nest
on the brick cliffs of our chimney stack
three hundred yards from the promenade;
and the first we'll know of it will be
when two pompoms of grey fluff
land on the half roof overlooked
by the photocopier and the fax machine.

And though the mother gull
will dive at us, squawking every time
she sees us dart from car to office door,
we'll watch as spring warms into summer
and the fledglings sleep and peck and flap their way
into adulthood, growing sleek grey feathers,
discarding the fluff of their infant lives.

Eyeing us through the glass, impatiently they'll pace
the five square yards of roof, measuring by hops
and runs and wingspans, readying for take-off.
Then some fine morning, we'll arrive to find one
not asleep but huddled, less, trying again
and again to shake his fractious feathers
into place; and again. All day

while the fax machine bleeps
and the photocopier hums away
we'll watch from our side of the window
one eye on the clock, knowing that at five
we'll pull down the blinds, switch off
the photocopier and leave the office,
avoiding the eye of the waiting mother bird.

Eleanor Livingstone

Heron Crossing

Bolted-together – bone crate
towed by the wind, always
seeming to fly backwards, till
you work out that head and neck
sunk into its thorax is the front end,
not the knobbed, trailing, elegant feet.

How can this Wright brothers'
primitive flying machine,
whose function is to test flight
at the edge of falling, turn,
skim down the runway of air to land,
become an icon
for the still gaze of water?

Kate Foley

Sandpiper

She is a speckle of feathers
dappled by shadows
of overhanging grasses,
          the only give-away
her black bead eye watching,
          watching.

Approach too close
and she's a flicker of wings,
a smooth arc swinging over water.

When she lands her legs are springs.
She's a bob, a curtsey,
and a long rippling whistle.

Her nest is a treasure chest,
her eggs satin-glossed, ink sploshed,
smooth as pearls.

On the day her first chick hatches
she's a demon, a vertical flight
of panic-stricken fluttering,
a crescendo
          of frantic warning cries.

Mavis Gulliver

Swans Over

Walking the water meadows
I saw
three swans flying broad formation
over town: flimsy bombers
gleaming in February light.
We should have crouched under tables,
scanned their flight, counting seconds.
But they carried, just,
enormous beauty
heavy in the feathered belly.
And nothing fell, but floated,
yellow bugle notes, gods' stories,
slow flap of horizons, snake's-ease.
And that interlay of down that warms
butted against the brown river, homely.

Pamela Coren

Sand Martins on the Rhymney

Swift-scooting along the gentle curve of the river,
Panicking sand martins, newly arrived from wherever,
Are looking out for short-term accommodation.
Bat-flittering hopefully against the retaining wall,
They peer into the open ends of drainage pipes –
'Hello-o! Anybody ho-ome?'

Our gullible ancestors used to believe that the swallows
Who dipped in long swoops to kiss the surface of water
Would, at the first sign of summer's ending,
Dive deep to lie warm in the comforting mud until spring.

For they do sound a bit far-fetched, these tales of migration
And standing here leaning on railings beside the Rhymney
I could convince myself without very much trouble
That the martins have dribbled forth from the ends of the
drainpipes,
Sucked out by the sunshine.

Ann Drysdale

Puffin

Funny face you draw
crowds to sit for hours on cliff tops
just to catch a glimpse

you are an icon
of the friendlier face
of wild sea creatures

waddling comically close to precipice edge
then when the wind is fiercest turning
to stare at the blank rock wall behind

when we see you sitting in the sunshine,
orange bill clashing merrily with pink
thrift, it's easy to imagine

you're smiling, forget
you're just a tasty morsel
for peregrines, black-backed gulls and skuas.

Chuckle on, sad clown,
buffeted by life but still contented,
full of charm.

Alwyn Marriage

The Company of the Preachers

(words taken from the RSPB website)

You recognise them
by their primitive appearance.
From rocky shores and estuaries,
long-necked, reptilian, black.

Regarded as sinister and greedy, they are
supreme fishers. Persecuted in the past
but over-wintering in numbers,
now coming to a gravel pit near you.

Cormorants. Expect conflict.

Joy Howard

Kingfisher

A shot - a bolt of brilliance not
from low green willows
by the minnowed shallows
but through a loveless stretch
where straggling branches snag
crisp packets, empty cartons, Safeway bags
and the rusting bars of trolleys trawl grey waters.

His back - just glimpsed - a snatch of
other skies. Bright lapis lazuli
fresh from the artist's slab of porphyry.
Ultramarine - blue from beyond my sea -
lent wings by some exotic deity
who stole the glow from summer orange groves
to fire the breast.

Kathryn Daszkiewicz

Heron on the Pier

Four times you came, four mornings,
blade-beaked grey dawn sentinel,
spindle-legged on mediaeval
stones. Four times you turned your back
on me, the academic gown
of feathers ruffled at your neck.
Stiff and unbending, you stared
balefully towards the sea,
hunchbacked, an old man grumping
at his incapacities.

I was surprised to see you
as a bird, so like yourself
I had no hesitation
in identifying you,
though I had hoped for closer
manifestations. The last
time you appeared, you swivelled
awkwardly, stared, nodded, dipped
your beak, saluting briefly
before taking to the air.

Lyn Moir

At the Edge of the Sea

The waves tug at the weed
Then comb its fronds on the sand,
Like stroking hands;
Here, where the sand is flat,
The curled pipings of surf swirl like ringlets
And the folded water
Sways and tumbles,
Humps up, teeters and melts:
A grin of white teeth for a moment.
The cries of terns force their grating locks:
One knifes down
Making a tiny cetacean spout
Then it swims its way
Out of the sea and up, oaring its wings,
Twisting a balancing tail,
Tightroping along the knotted air.

Upright and still,
A young man stares at all this;
Tranced by the tern, by the breathing sea.

Hermione Sandall

Air

Flight Path

An incoming shadow
combing the deckled fields
before the tarmac strip. And growing.

A flock of starlings.

Which speckled bird could anticipate
the impact from that silver roar
claiming the airspace as its own?
Would have left soft-beaked nestlings –
little bowls of crocuses –
hidden in shady tree holes?

I imagine one starling,
then, wing-tip to wing-tip, a throng
spinning like tossed mussel shells
or a broken nib spattering the sky.

Ladders. Masks. Elbow-length gloves.

Technicians clamber through intakes,
stuff sack after songless sack
while a more silent day
leans its head against clouds.

Pat Borthwick

Swallows

Surprised by such proximity
I note the chestnut brow and throat,
the black-blue wings, the threads
of trailing tail, and wonder where
their nest is. Unused to parleying
with birds and they to me, eyeball
to eyeball, a dialogue of sorts
ensues, a non-aggression pact
whereby I'm free to watch, admire
their grace, their charm, their colouring
and they acquire from me the lease
for building of a temporary base,
sheltered, sea view, rent-free.

Lyn Moir

The Arrival of the Swifts

Not dusk, so much,
as a dilating to the light.
the garden a calyx,
the sepals peeled back

where we stand, looking up.
Heart's corolla
open to the blue.
Watching the swifts.

Can you see them circling,
sewing the clouds
with high pitched cries,
the thin scream of summer?

Over roofs' red shoals,
over the tip of the tallest ash
as they soar, dive,
skate in the void?

Children of the zenith,
electrons dancing,
it's said they'll be
on the wing all night.

Breasting stars
we can hardly see,
the faceless ionospheric
face of the deep:
joy's calligraphy.

Lynne Wycherley

Skylark

Suddenly above the fields you're pouring
Pure joy in a shower of bubbles,
Lacing the spring with the blue thread of summer.
You're the warmth of the sun in a song.

You're light spun to a fine filament;
Sun on a spider-thread -
That delicate.

You're the lift and balance the soul feels,
The terrible, tremulous, uncertain thrill of it -
You're all the music the heart needs,
Full of its sudden fall, silent fields.

Katrina Porteous

Starlings at 9 a.m.

Oiled snakeskin dagger-heads
shiny macks flashing the sun

the gang's here with its click and whistle
stab and damson-guzzle muttering

in a louche phalanx of swarthy style
short swords and thonged feet

one screwdriver hammering throat
to a leaf, a hidden racket tree

but each braille-texted breast
whirrs for its sleek greenbottle self

and that plum speared in the beak.
Hard to shake: in the ear like wax and pins.

9.15 are you going out   stab
or are you   not   going out?

Pamela Coren

Flit

An hour after sunset
when the dor beetle flies
a nightjar wheels and glides

quite noiseless on a warm
and windless night.

Evejar, wheelbird,
moth owl, spinner…
his plumage is leaf-shadow,
mottle of bark and darkness.

Fern hawk, lich fowl, chaffer…
his call an unearthly churr.

In Nidderdale
folk said the souls
of infants unbaptised
passed into nightjars:

birds whose gaping beaks
retain the wide, black, yawn
of an abandoned chick.

Kathryn Daszkiewicz

On the Aerial

Starling is numerous, holds in his throat
The many colours of his oily coat.
Each year he - like his fathers - finds new noise,
Wolf-whistles tall as boys,
The phone's trill, then the shriek
Of Kirsty, loudest child in all our street.
Tonight he softly mews. Then through his voice are poured
Jay, blackbird's honey, thrush-lilts. He, half-heard,
Tilts at faint stars, is spring, is every bird.

Alison Brackenbury

Kestrel

Kestrel, small masterful falcon: I'd have you
nothing beyond yourself. Let me not see you
as symbol; no minion; your shudder
on the tilting air never the posture
of a servant before his lord.

That outsling from the clough, traverse, brilliant
plunge and rise from the soaked grass
with laden talons, hunger taught
at the rim of a charnel nest.
Wild blood's the apple of your perfect eye.

M R Peacocke

House Martins

Scarcely a minute
I do not think of them, those loop-
the-loop pilots in gunmetal and the purest of white,
ranked tight on the telephone wires,
not even room for a single *chichirrp* between them.
A latecomer adds his tiny weight
to the end of the row, twitter-rippling the line
with a Mexican wave of sound until every wing
is resettled, each feather lies calmed.
Perhaps the hum of conversation backwards
and forwards beneath their feet is warming.
I passed below them yesterday
as I pulled out from the milking yard,
and nudged my way through tail-flicking Friesians
on their nonchalant amble back to the field.
They hardly noticed my car,
nor my house martins festooned
in long scalloped curves
despite the northerly wind,
the strengthening wind,
the wind they had their backs to.
This morning, no acrobatics
over the barn, no skimming the tops of trees,
and I knew I would never see them again,
not a single one, until next year's warmth
dizzies the meadows and river banks with
fidgety flies, exposes mud to wattle and daub
the winter gaps in their half-bowl English homes.
I imagine them now
flocking out just ahead of the frost,
crossing the Cornish coast then drawn on and into
the sun's raw warmth as it overslopes the equator.
In a week, I will email or ring
all of Gibraltar, North Africa, Southern Spain
and ask them to look out and up
through their sky-blue windows.
Then call me back.

Pat Borthwick

Skylark Rising

It pauses, then with a push of wings
swims upwards through the air,
all the time singing,
scattering notes like bright pennies,
bold in the copper sky.

Soon its lifting silhouette is gone.
All you can see now is the song.

Gill McEvoy

Shadows in Japonica Lane

The swifts have gone, their summer screams erased.
Black small-time scimitars have cut the sky.

Now swallows, silent, are on standby, glazed
by yellow light, recalling how to fly

their far-flung course. Above the sedge they queue
in dots and dashes, decking out the wires.

They used to plunge like anchors falling through
the sapphire, diving low past clouds and spires

as if their medium was the sea, not air.
Now soon they'll lift off rolling one by one.

Above the bronzing trees massed flags will flare
away from darkening land towards the sun.

They'll chain the sky in loops without regret.
While skittering leaves are sighing to the earth,

as frail and twisted thoughts one can't forget,
in topaz, ruby stains to show rebirth

of jewel colours on the edge of death.
The fleshy plums are purpled, dropped, wasp-blown,

and frets of frost are mingled with the breath
of autumn. Spiders, urgently, alone,

are busy linking stems and meshing traps.
A mist comes creeping like a maiden aunt,

all fat and sheepish spreading out in gaps
to muffle village children's skipping chant

as down the lane they make a dreamlike frieze
in black and white below the dripping trees.

Jenny Morris

Another Life

"like to the swift flight of a sparrow through the room
wherein you sit" *The Venerable Bede*

Left alone up there in the dark
the starling would have gone
quietly, huddled against a box
of Christmas decorations

a few late flutterings causing
tiny bells to ring out of season,
the iridescence of his wings
fading to a dusty black

but we threw open the hatch,
rattled the Ramsay ladder
and startled him into wild panic

nothing straightforward
about his sojourn here
except that final mad flight.

Eleanor Livingstone

Loss of Swifts

I have lost them.
It is the last thing I think before sleep comes
And the first on waking.

They came back.
Meeting in the sky high above the valley
And homing in on the place they knew as theirs.

But it was not as they had left it.
A couple of passes up and down the terrace,
A look at the altered hole, the expensive nest-box
And they were gone again.

The Council put the ultimatum in writing;
It *had to be done*. Shifting the blame helps
But it doesn't stop me thinking about them, imagining,
Needing to know if their grief is as great as mine.

Over and over *mea culpa, mea maxima culpa*

While the swifts cry high in the hot air over the valley
And I sit willing them, wishing them, wanting them back.

I need to know how to tell it to start sanding down
The lump of regret standing proud of the smooth summer;
Guddling in my head for the words to make it right –

> *They were tourists, unsatisfied with the changed arrangements*
> *They have simply decided to take their custom elsewhere.*
> *You must come to terms with your having lost the contract*
> *Despite your high-profile attention to customer care…*

They will be all right. They will have found somewhere better.
They have only voted against me with their feet.
Their dear soft skinny inadequate lovable feet.

Ann Drysdale

Choughs at Kinsale

Rose-thorns lit by sunlight,
their red legs glow
with the fire of glass
as they hook into the air,

then fall,
so steep and bold
our hearts forget
to beat.

Gill McEvoy

Swallow in Autumn

There is gold, there is brown;
there is mazy line pattern.
I skim the zigzag field, dip
the slide of the river
downswoop to silver
there is bright, there is shadow;
blue glass shine. I flick
flicker, downtwist the spine
of the valley. Here is cloud under
and wet gleam of rain.

Jo Haslam

Take Off

Rough stubble glows, burnt apricot.
A buzzard soars. Light clings.
His breast a travelling sunset,
He warms the world with wings.

Alison Brackenbury

The Reality of Eagles

Nothing can prepare us for eagles,
the reality of them,
their indifference,
the grandeur of their wings,
how they subjugate the air
and the space between mountains,
shadows hovering
between us and the sun.

Angela Kirby

Air Raid

Each after each
the pigeons rise in difficulty,
turn a raggedy edge to the wind
and sail a clean arc,
signing the sky effortless.
Crows bucket into the wind.
The sparrowhawk unwraps
a great bar above the land.
His golden flag drops every bird
secret and soft into twig and tree,
small speech of the fields
silent under the predatory word.
When he peters off in his eternal boredom
voices are given back, flight resumes.

Twice he has killed and eaten
in my garden. Once I went out to him
and he stared from his brash heraldry.
He held my gaze until I could have
reached out and swatted him,
but at my finger's end he rose,
clamped on the bloody breast meat
and lifted his scattering feast
back into the effortless sky.

Pamela Coren

The Garden at Dusk

There's not a whisper of wind so you stand there,
holding clothes in your arms, a familiar yearning
opening to welcome every rustle, the velvet light.
There's no breeze, so why the sheet of newspaper
floating past your ear? An owl assembles himself
on the clothes post, a white owl whose wide eyes
take you in like washing – he's grave, composed.
Although you stay stone still he flies too soon –
you lose him to a smudge of trees beyond the wall.
Summer evenings you leave the light off, watching.

Irene Rawnsley

On Kestrel Ridge

We have come beyond the places
where painted signs tell walkers
where to look, what to see.
The trails across the tussocked
land are too narrow for boots
and straight as the fox's
bloody thought.

Grey geese chevron the sky
and a kestrel hangs,
kites on the wind, waits
for a neon scurry to spark
in her eye, our movements
too large for notice.

Wind bends the grass,
shivers it from green to silver.
We have to go on, go further:
the paths down are behind us.
They are steep and hidden.

Angela France

Late Road Home

Nothing can erase that pale owl
moored on the metal,
the way he turned his bonneted head
to challenge my headlights.
Beak, talons, pole star bright.
A blood red moon in his full crop.
Then, like the sure hauling of sails
for a long outward passage,
he hauled his quiet featheriness
up and into the encircling night.
Wingbeats as sure, as silent,
as this road home,
away from you.

Pat Borthwick

Raven

He clasps the mast with a cricketer's fingers
High up among the paraphernalia
Of media coverage and mobile phones.
He attracts my attention. *Er – ahem –*
You there – 'scuse me – wassatime?

Throaty croak hinting at late nights and fag-smoke.
A young executive in a good black suit;
Too bad he slept in it. Stretching and flexing,
He is pulling it back into some semblance of shape
As we speak.

His jowl bristles.
He has not shaved today – designer stubble
Taken to unacceptable extremes; he is pushing his luck.
Now, ready as he'll ever be, he takes the plunge,
Flies on a straight steady line to the Black Mountains.

Lazily following the valley, he stays with the gradient
To the top of a long, slow loop. Then suddenly –
Aaagh, fuck! – as he realises he's on the wrong train.
A dive sideways. Trailing at arms' length umbrella, briefcase,
raincoat,
He streaks for the Beacons.

Ann Drysdale

January Sky with Red Kites

Your five-foot wingspan prints the sky,
a red colophon on vellum,
fire-spirit in a lead-drizzled day.

Cardinal, king of the reds,
the russet woods, these Chiltern bricks.
Taut, elated, swerving,

seeming to need
nothing but air while we
drag laptop and raincoat, shrink-wrap and tins,
worries on our backs, Waitrose in our hands.

At Ivinghoe Beacon your wild flags fly –
Wendover, Towersey –
our footsteps beating softly
under your blood.

All day your outline swoops and turns.
I see your auburn banner and I burn.

Lynne Wycherley

August 1950

A dark cloud on the right, swerving and weaving
in figures of eight over the evening woods
forming, re-forming - sashes and ribbons
plaiting a monochrome dance, high in the air.

Grandfather, father, child, we stand in the road:
too far for the whirr, the beat of wings to reach us
out of the high oscillations inside the cloud –
not a screech from the beaks, not a yawp, not a burble.

On their unseen dance floor the starlings shimmy
partnered by thousands, wing-tip to wing-tip, a feather's
width away, but never clipping or brushing
even a filament... And the cloud unravels.

We turn to each other, and find we are standing on tiptoe.

Christine Webb

Endpiece

The Bird

How its head vibrates, the beak
braced on a song that flows
without hesitation from depths
of time toward depths of time.

Sounds to be lived by. Like feathers
with nothing to choose but keep skin
sheathed, bones able to fly.
Aware, though not self-aware.

I envy that. But at once
a consciousness echoes in mine –
one which discovered self
as miracle, riches of isolation.

What right have I, late come,
not to use words, not cast
phrase after phrase in search
of a world by that gift made strange?

The bird, running through his beak
a long flight-feather, sits
clear of these words – but, for me,
seen partly through if beyond them.

Anne Cluysenaar

Index of Poets

Index of Birds

The Poets

Lynn Alderson 'I live in West Yorkshire, in spite of the weather. Animals and birds are a great source of joy in my life. Especially birds, as they are not only beautiful, but part of the truly wild to which we are sometimes able to come close.'

Alison Brackenbury's seventh collection is *Singing in the Dark*, Carcanet. She has recently produced a chapbook of animal poems, *Shadow*, available from HappenStance Press. New poems can be read at her website: www.alisonbrackenbury.co.uk. As a child, she lived in a house in a wood, where she met more birds than people.

Pat Borthwick has three full-length collections, *Admiral FitzRoy's Barometer* (Templar, 2008) being her most recent. She is the GPS co-ordinator for East Yorkshire, a Hawthornden Fellow and Senior Tutor for the OCA. She has 720 birds featured in artwork around her house! Pat's personal dream is to see a bittern.

Carole Bromley lives in York where she teaches creative writing at the University's Centre for Lifelong Learning. Widely published, she has two pamphlets from Smith/Doorstop, *Unscheduled Halt* (2005) and *Skylight* (2009). Carole tempts as many different birds as she can into her town garden.

Marianne Burton's pamphlet *The Devil's Cut* was a PBS Choice. Her poem 'For A Plain Man' won the *Mslexia* poetry competition, and a full collection is forthcoming from Seren. She is widely published in magazines, including *Agenda, Chapman, Poetry London, Poetry Wales, The Rialto, Stand,* and *TLS*. She is a passionate bird enthusiast.

A C Clarke has published *The Gallery on the Left* (Akros Press 2003), *Breathing Each Other In* (Blinking Eye Publishers 2005), *Messages of Change* (Oversteps Books 2008). The otherness of birds, whether seen in the countryside or a city backyard, has always fascinated her. Like us they are two-legged and hot-blooded!

Anne Cluysenaar's new and selected, *Timeslips*, appeared from Carcanet (1997); more recently, the book-length sequence *Batu-Angas: Envisioning Nature with Alfred Russel Wallace*, Seren, 2008, and a group of autobiographical poems *Water to Breathe*, Flarestack, 2009. Forthcoming from Cinnamon: *Migrations*. Birds inhabit much of her work, helping compose 'a secret...which breathes itself in us'.

Pamela Coren taught English Literature at the University of Leicester until retiring in 2000. She has published in many magazines and won some prizes. Her first collection, *The Blackbird Inspector,* was published by Laurel Books in 2005. She lives in Stamford, along with an abundance of sparrows, thrushes and skylarks.

Kathryn Daszkiewicz lives and works in Lincolnshire. She was awarded a writer's bursary by East Midlands Arts in 2001. *In the Dangerous Cloakroom,* her first full-length collection, was published by Shoestring Press in October 2006. Ornithology has been one of her interests from childhood, inspired by her father.

Ann Drysdale lives in South Wales and has been a hill farmer, water-gypsy, countryside columnist and single parent - not necessarily in that order. Birds have enriched her many lives, as neighbours, friends, wandering minstrels and treasured responsibilities. They appear, in these and other guises, in her five collections of poetry.

Fiona Durance has worked in dance, music, equalities training and as a BSL interpreter. Her work has appeared in magazines and anthologies, in theatres, galleries and on radio. Her writing has been placed in several international competitions. Wild birds' beauty, songs and perky personalities always make her smile.

Kate Foley's first collection was shortlisted for the Aldeburgh best first collection prize. Her fifth is in preparation. She claims no special knowledge of birds but feels that to bring one alive on the page for the reader to 'watch' is one of the most satisfying - and tough - jobs for a poet.

Angela France is a Gloucestershire-based poet. Her second collection is *Occupation* (Ragged Raven Press 2010). She has had poems published in many leading journals in the UK and the USA, and has been frequently anthologised. 'Birds colour my morning walks and lift the darkest of days; I can't imagine a sky without them.

Mavis Gulliver writes mainly of islands and wildlife. Over sixty of her poems have appeared in poetry magazines such as *Envoi, Iota* and *Poetry Scotland.* Her home is in the Hebrides and she writes, and observes a wealth of birdlife, from a log cabin just ten metres above the sea.

Jo Haslam is published by Smith/Doorstep Books. Her work has appeared in many poetry magazines including *The Rialto, Ambit,* and *The North,* and has been placed in The National Poetry, Yorkshire Open and Lancaster Literature Festival competitions. Bird behaviour and the mythology surrounding them both feature in her work.

Joy Howard has lived in West Yorkshire since 1987; poetry has always been part of her life. On retirement she took the opportunity to make it central, and co-founded Grey Hen Press in 2008. Compiling the poems for this book has been both an education and a delight.

Angela Kirby grew up in rural Lancashire, where her father taught her to recognise and name favourite birds of woodland and garden. Her poems are widely published and she was the BBC's Wildlife Poet of the Year in 1995 and 2001. Her collections *Mr. Irresistible* and *Dirty Work* (Shoestring Press) have just been reprinted.

Gill Learner has been widely published and has won a number of awards including the Poetry Society's Hamish Canham Prize 2008. She writes at a desk overlooking the garden and is easily distracted by avian activity, from blackbirds splashing in the birdbath to red kites planing overhead.

Eleanor Livingstone is Director of StAnza, Scotland's International Poetry Festival. Her own most recent collection, *Even the Sea* (Red Squirrel Press), includes many poems featuring birds. Not for her the rare or exotic, rather she writes about the seagulls, starlings and pigeons who inhabit the margins of our daily stops and starts.

Gill McEvoy Pamphlets: *Uncertain Days* and *A Sampler* (HappenStance Press 2006, 2008). (Cinnamon Press 2010). Online at redbotinki.blogpost.com and www.poemcatchers.com. Gill was a BTO volunteer counter (survey of wading birds on the Mersey estuary). Birds feature in many of her poems. Observing birds and hearing birdsong are the stuff of life.

Alwyn Marriage has six collections; her poetry has also appeared in numerous magazines and anthologies. She is Managing Editor of Oversteps Books and a Visiting Fellow at the University of Surrey. Having tracked down only the occasional puffin, she was thrilled to find herself surrounded by several hundred in the Shetlands. Online at www.marriages.me.uk.

Lyn Moir, born in Scotland in 1934, has published collections with Arrowhead in 2001 and 2003. Calder Wood Press published *Easterly, Force 10* in 2009 and will publish her fourth, *Velázquez's Riddle*, in 2011. She lives in St Andrews, on the harbour, where seabirds are her constant companions.

Jenny Morris writes poems and fiction. Her writing has won awards and appeared in many magazines and anthologies (including *A Twist of Malice* and *Cracking On*). Her latest poetry collection is *Lunatic Moon*. She lives in Norfolk where bitterns boom in the reedbeds.

Hilary J Murray is a founder member of Borderstone Poets, Leeds; co-founder of Yorkshire women's poetry network EPIC. Her poems feature in *Second Bite* and *A Twist of Malice* (Grey Hen Press). As a child in Kent she sometimes heard a cuckoo, far away beyond the apple orchards.

Meg Peacocke 'I'm working on my fifth collection. Blackbirds pecking at red apples on the grass: I asked my mother for a little bag of salt to sprinkle on their tails. I was three; I've watched birds ever since (though not wanting to catch them).'

Katrina Porteous lives at the edge of land, sea and sky on the Northumberland coast, where she envies the birds their movement between elements. She is best known for her poems for BBC Radio and her publications include *The Lost Music, Dunstanburgh, Longshore Drift* and *The Blue Lonnen.* Website: www.katrinaporteous.co.uk.

Joan Poulson, poet and children's writer, trained as a ceramicist, has collaborated with artists across genres, held several land-art residencies, and looks forward to more work outdoors, particularly to further projects involving trees and bird-life, to celebrating her passion for the natural world.

Irene Rawnsley is a prize-winning poet who lives in Settle where she is woken by jackdaws every morning. She has published six books of poetry, including three for children. A new collection from Smith Doorstop is due out next year.

Hermione Sandall is retired: she sails in summer and does voluntary conservation work in winter. She is a contributor to *Cracking On,* Grey Hen's recent anthology of poems on ageing. Her interests are language, music, and the natural world, birds in particular.

Gina Shaw lived in the country until she was twelve. When the family moved to town she grieved for the countryside. She has always felt uplifted by the natural world. Why birds? First, their great variety. Second, the things they can do, and all without hands. Third - why not birds, they can fly.

Christine Webb's collection *After Babel* was published in 2004 by Peterloo Poets. In 2007 her poem 'Seven Weeks' won the *Poetry London* competition, and last year she completed a Creative Writing MA. An RSPB member, she enjoys varied species - from goldcrests to red kites - visiting or overflying her garden.

Lynne Wycherley used to work in wildlife conservation: images of nature, birds, and landscape occur throughout her poetry. Her recent poetry books *North Flight* (from the Fens to Iceland) and *Poppy in a Storm-Struck Field* (partly in memory of her mother) are available from Shoestring Press.

The Illustrator

Emma Stansfield was born in 1972. She studied Wildlife Illustration at Carmarthenshire College of Technology and Art, and subsequently gained an MA in Natural History Illustration at the Royal College of Art. She lives and works with her husband and their son at the Bird Observatory on Bardsey Island off the coast of Wales.

Acknowledgements

PAT BORTHWICK 'Late Road Home' and 'House Martins' (from sequence 'Hospital Corners') *Swim* (Mudfog 2005). ALISON BRACKENBURY 'Take Off' published in *Snakeskin* and *Poems in the Waiting Room 2009*; 'On the Aerial' *Shadow* (HappenStance Press 2009), also published in *Staple* and *Bards in the Bog* (Shetland Public Libraries 2009). CAROLE BROMLEY 'Hedge Sparrows' online publication, *Guardian Poetry Workshop*. MARIANNE BURTON 'Sparrowhawk' published in *Smiths Knoll*. A C CLARKE 'Assembly of Birds' *Messages of Change* (Oversteps Books 2008); also published in *The Interpreter's House*. ANNE CLUYSENAAR 'The Bird' published in *ARTEMISpoetry*. PAMELA COREN 'Starlings at 9 a.m.', 'New Season's Blackbird' and 'Swans Over' published in *Raindog*; 'When the Wren Sings' published in *The Rialto*. ANN DRYSDALE 'Raven' and 'Loss of Swifts' *Backwork* (Peterloo Poets 2002); 'Mallard' and 'Sand Martins on the Rhymney' *Between Dryden and Duffy* (Peterloo Poets 2005). KATE FOLEY 'Heron Crossing' (as 'Heron') and 'Hawk on a Chimney Pot' *A Year without Apricots* (Blackwater Press, 1999). ANGELA FRANCE 'On Kestrel Ridge' *Occupation* (Ragged Raven Press 2009); 'The Wren Doesn't Wait for May' published in *Poetry Monthly*. MAVIS GULLIVER 'Waymarks' and 'Sandpiper' published in *Envoi*. JO HASLAM 'Swallow in Autumn' *Lunar Moths* (Smith/Doorstop 2005). ANGELA KIRBY 'The Reality of Eagles' *Poems on the Buses* 2001. ELEANOR LIVINGSTONE 'How to Watch A Seagull' and 'Another Life' *Even the Sea* (Red Squirrel Press 2010). GILL McEVOY 'Choughs at Kinsale' published in *Envoi*; 'Skylark Rising' published in *Poetry Scotland*; 'Heron' published in *Nth Position*. LYN MOIR 'Swallows' and 'Bodybuilding for Beginners' *Easterly, Force 10* (Calder Wood Press 2009). HILARY J MURRAY 'In the Wild' *Second Bite* (Grey Hen Press 2008). M R PEACOCKE 'Haiku' features in Kirkby Stephen's *Poetry Path*; 'Kestrel' *In Praise of Aunts* (Peterloo Poets 2008). KATRINA PORTEOUS 'Skylark' *The Lost Music* (Bloodaxe Books, 1996); 'Kittiwakes': extract from *Dunstanburgh* (Smokestack Books 2004, originally a commission for BBC Radio 4); 'Brent Geese': extract from *The Refuge Box*, commissioned for BBC Radio 3 in 2007. IRENE RAWNSLEY 'The Garden at Dusk', published in *Smiths Knoll*. GINA SHAW 'Dunnock' *Second Bite* (Grey Hen Press 2008). CHRISTINE WEBB 'August 1950' *After Babel* (Peterloo Poets, 2004); 'Rooks in February' published in *Smiths Knoll*. LYNNE WYCHERLEY 'Bewick's Swans Arrive at Ouse Washes' *At the Edge of Light* (Shoestring Press 2003); 'January Sky with Red Kites' published in *The Frogmore Papers*; 'The Arrival of the Swifts' published in *Agenda*; 'The Arctic Terns of Northmavine' published in *The New Shetlander*; 'Manx Shearwaters' in the Oxford anthology *East of Auden* (Poetry Direct, 2003).

Grey Hen Press is dedicated to publishing the work of older women. It is for this reason that all the poems in this book are by women whose ages range from forty to eighty plus. That these poems are worth reading is however nothing to do with age or gender and everything to do with the ability to write a fine poem.

The title of this book is taken from Ann Drysdale's poem 'The Poet and the Long-Tailed Tit'.

Joy Howard is a co-founder of Grey Hen Press. Her poems were widely anthologised in the '80s and '90s. She is a contributor to Grey Hen's first publication *Second Bite* and to both subsequent anthologies *A Twist of Malice* (2008) and *Cracking On* (2009). She has also published a collection of poems *Exit Moonshine* (Grey Hen 2009) about her 'coming out' experiences in the 1980s. Shortlisted in several competitions, she was a Chapter One Open Poetry prizewinner in 2007, and has been recently published in *Sofia, Sphinx, The Interpreter's House* and *ARTEMISpoetry.* Her poems can be found online at *Guardian Unlimited* and *poetry p f,* and feature in *Poems While You Wait* at St James's Hospital in Leeds. Her work has been selected for a new anthology from Headland Publications, due out in 2010.

www.greyhenpress.com